Ten Ways to Share Your Faith in the Workplace Without Saying a Word

By

Rob Bowles

Edited by Diane Rowley and Patty Drake
Cover Designed by Brooke Bowles

toc

Table of Contents

Foreward

Obviously, God's desires for us to verbally share the gospel, but He also wants us to communicate the good news through the actions of our life. God tells us to live such good lives that even those who accuse us of doing wrong will see our good deeds and glorify Him on the day He visits. He instructs wives to win over their unbelieving husbands without using words but through the purity and reverence of their behavior. If our faith in God shows up in the way we work, then we will bear fruit for the gospel in doing our jobs. Every day, God wants our lives along with our words to proclaim His good news to our family, friends, and coworkers.

> 1 Corinthians 15:1-6 Now, brothers, I want to remind you of the gospel I preached to you, which you received and on which you have taken your stand. By this gospel you are saved, if you hold firmly to the word I preached to you. Otherwise, you have believed in vain. For what I received I passed on to you as of first importance: that Christ died for our sins according to the Scriptures, that he was buried, that he was raised on the third day according to the Scriptures, and that he appeared to Peter, and then to the Twelve. After that, he appeared to more than five hundred of the brothers at the same time, most of whom are still living, though some have fallen asleep.

> 1 Peter 2:12 Live such good lives among the pagans that, though they accuse you of doing wrong, they may see your good deeds and glorify God on the day he visits us.

> 1 Peter 3:1-2 Wives, in the same way be submissive to your husbands so that, if any of them do not believe the word, they may be won over without words by the behavior of their wives, when they see the purity and reverence of your lives.

> Colossians 4:5-6 Be wise in the way you act towards outsiders; make the most of every opportunity. Let your conversation be always full of grace, seasoned with salt, so that you may know how to answer everyone.

i

Introduction

Jesus touched people's lives by the way He lived. Jesus not only spoke the truth to those who were listening but He lived out the truth to a world that was watching. His life harmonized with His words and moved individuals and the masses to seek Him out. Jesus was kind, compassionate, and giving as He healed, fed, and forgave people. The actions of His life are a beacon of love that leads us to Him. We learn from Jesus that what we do matters just as much as what we say. This is especially true at work, where people are watching to see if we swim like the fish on our bumper. God knows we make it difficult for our coworkers to believe that His love keeps no record of wrongs if were always gossiping about other employees. Every lie we tell and grudge we hold causes our teammates to doubt that the truth can really set them free. I know for myself, too many times my behavior only taught my teammates about the fallen nature of man, rather than exhibiting any of the characteristics of God. Obviously, God is hoping for something better. He wants our office to be a sanctuary for the coworkers who avoided Him on Sunday to encounter Him in us throughout the week. Pleasing God by the way we work is how we lead the congregation of people that meets in our workplace into worshiping Him too.

John 1:1,14 In the beginning was the Word, and the Word was with God, and the Word was God. The Word became flesh and made his dwelling among us. We have seen his glory, the glory of the One and Only, who came from the Father, full of grace and truth.

Philippians 2:12-16 Therefore, my dear friends, as you have always obeyed--not only in my presence, but now much more in my absence--continue to work out your salvation with fear and trembling, for it is God who works in you to will and to act according to his good purpose. Do everything without complaining or arguing, so that you may become blameless and pure, children of God without fault in a crooked and depraved generation, in which you shine like stars in the universe as you hold out the word of life--in order that I may boast on the day of Christ that I did not run or labor for nothing.

Romans 12:1 Therefore, I urge you, brothers, in view of God's mercy, to offer your bodies as living sacrifices, holy and pleasing to God--this is your spiritual act of worship.

God gives divine purpose, personal fulfillment, and a better night's sleep to any job when our main concern is to humbly serve Him. We are called to be God's ambassadors and every job, project, and assignment is a chance to represent Him by our attitude, words, and deeds. God helps us fulfill our calling by giving us His Spirit to teach us His ways and empower us to take what we've learned at church and apply it in our workplace. If the fruit of His Spirit is displayed in our actions, then seeds of faith will be sown into the hearts of our coworkers. Every time we act with kindness, self-discipline, and boldness of faith we glorify God in our office and draw our teammates to Him. We don't need to book a conference room to explain how God forgives sinners; we can get the conversation started by simply admitting our mistakes rather than denying them. An honest and sincere apology is a great way to express our faith in God's grace to the employee who thinks that they need to earn their way into heaven. Obviously, we can't make our teammates go to church to learn about the love of God but no one will stop us from working in ways that let them experience His love through us.

> 2 Corinthians 5:18-20 All this is from God, who reconciled us to himself through Christ and gave us the ministry of reconciliation: that God was reconciling the world to himself in Christ, not counting men's sins against them. And he has committed to us the message of reconciliation. We are therefore Christ's ambassadors, as though God were making his appeal through us. We implore you on Christ's behalf: Be reconciled to God.

> Isaiah 66:2 Has not my hand made all these things, and so they came into being?" declares the LORD. "This is the one I esteem: he who is humble and contrite in spirit, and trembles at my word."

All of us can get our priorities out of order and this book is meant to encourage us to work in ways that will bless us and make God known to others. If we will let God align our perspective with His Word, then we'll be able to see the changes He wants to make in us. Transformation happens when we believe that God loves us just the way we are and actively trust that His ways are better than ours. We don't have to be flawless to start walking with God; we simply need to be willing to be led by the One who promises to make us perfect. In writing this book, the Lord brought to my attention some of the times that I let my pride, greed, and insecurity get the best of me. I've added a few of my weak faith moments to let you see how silly and shortsided it is to not trust in God while doing our jobs.

> Hebrews 10:24-25 And let us consider how we may spur one another on towards love and good deeds. Let us not give up meeting together, as some are in the habit of doing, but let us encourage one another--and all the more as you see the Day approaching.

This book is perfect for small groups to read together and go through the questions at the end of each chapter. I suggest taking turns reading out loud the chapter and starting the conversation by asking if anyone wants to comment on anything that spoke to them. Then, go through the questions. I've included example answers (real responses not necessary the right ones) to help get everyone thinking. Please ask God to reveal to yourself how you really respond and interact at work before you answer. I know for myself, sometimes I can be quick to respond with what I should be doing and not what I actually do. Remember, God works through our admission and confession to lead us into repentance and change for our life. Listening to our friends without judging, sharing the truth about us, and praying for each other will encourage everyone to open up and let Jesus go to work in our lives.

Okay, enough of the introduction, let's look at ten ways we can share our faith in the workplace (also in our families, neighborhoods, churches, sport teams, and schools) without saying a word.

Questions for Reflection

1. Do your coworkers see God in you by the way you work? Have you asked God if they do? Can you share a moment when you did and a time you didn't demonstrate godliness?
Examples:
   - Sometimes yes, sometimes no.
   - I actually haven't asked God what my coworkers see in me.
   - The time I yelled and then apologized.

2. Who do you serve first at work? Can you think of a project or situation that shows your allegiance?
Examples:
   - Myself – I always do what I think is best for my career even if it's wrong in God's eyes.

- My Boss – I do what my boss tells me to do regardless if it's right or wrong.
- God – I work to please Him.

3. What is your top priority for your job? (Think of what get's you upset or happy – what you talk about when you come home.)
Examples:
- Make more money.
- Get more power and recognition.
- Work in a way that is pleasing to God and share His love with others.

4. How do your priorities affect the way you do your job?
Examples:
- Striving for money and recognition will lead to wrong behavior.
- When my top priority is to serve my boss then I am held to his standards.
- When I serve God I do good work whether I'm recognized for it or not.

5. When was the last time you said you were wrong at work or I'm sorry?
Examples:
- Never, yesterday, years ago

1

Work Expecting God's Favor

The path to success is paved with both opportunities and land mines. One right move sends us on the fast track; one wrong step and we're escorted to the door. It can be hard to determine whether a project will boost our career or sink it. We must carefully interact with bosses, peers, and customers who can explode when something goes wrong. We live with the pressure of knowing that one strategic mistake can cost us everything we've worked so hard to gain. It's difficult not to stress out over all the potential pitfalls at work, but in doing so we exchange the gift of God's favor for the fear of failure. Forgetting that God is able to use all things for our good gets us obsessing on everything that could go wrong. While it's true that many things can do damage to our career, God doesn't want us worrying about who or what's against us. God knows that we won't inspire our coworkers to trust in Him if they see we have no confidence in Him ourselves. Nobody sees our faith in Jesus if we're pessimistic and completely risk adverse. Since we can do all things through Christ, we have no reason not to pursue the impossible desires that God puts on our hearts. If we want to encourage our unsaved coworkers to reconsider their unbelief, then we need to let them see God do amazing things through us. God's favor is all about His goodness, not ours. None of us deserve it, but God is glorified in our workplace when we act upon it.

Romans 8:31 What, then, shall we say in response to this? If God is for us, who can be against us?

Psalms 37:4 Delight yourself in the LORD and he will give you the desires of your heart.

Philippians 4:13 I can do everything through him who gives me strength.

Psalms 5:12 For surely, O LORD, you bless the righteous; you surround them with your favor as with a shield.

Imagine if the owner or CEO of your company called you into their office and said that they thought of you like a son or daughter and wanted to help you with your career. After a second to let their words sink in, they go on to tell you that they've been watching you work and also providing the resources you've needed to be successful. A smile goes across their face as they explain that they have great plans for you. Then, they warmly tell you that if you ever need anything to not hesitate to give them a call. Yes, that's an incredible daydream, but if it really happened would it change the way you work? It shouldn't if you're a child of God because His kids already have His favor. We need to realize that our heavenly Father can't stop Himself from wanting to help us achieve the plans He has for our lives. Yet, like a stubborn teenager, we can give God the Heisman and limit His involvement by not taking Him up on His offer to equip us with everything we need for doing His will. I cringe to think about how many times I let my pride (I don't need God's help) or insecurity (Why would God help me?) keep me from seeking God's assistance. Relying on myself only hampered my success and kept God from achieving much greater things through me. Fatherhood has helped me understand how God must feel when we don't seek His favor. I know I'm hurt when my kid's don't believe I want to help them and a little insulted each time they think that I can't. If earthly dads go out of their way to support their children, then think about what our heavenly Father desires to do for us.

Hebrews 11:6 And without faith it is impossible to please God, because anyone who comes to him must believe that he exists and that he rewards those who earnestly seek him.

Matthew 7:7-11 "Ask and it will be given to you; seek and you will find; knock and the door will be opened to you. For everyone who asks receives; he who seeks finds; and to him who knocks, the door will be opened. "Which of you, if his son asks for bread, will give him a stone? Or if he asks for a fish, will give him a snake? If you, then, though you are evil, know how to give good gifts to your children, how much more will your Father in heaven give good gifts to those who ask him!

James 1:5-8 If any of you lacks wisdom, he should ask God, who gives generously to all without finding fault, and it will be given to him. But when he asks, he must believe and not doubt, because he who doubts is like a wave of the sea, blown and tossed by the wind. That man should not think he will receive anything from the Lord; he is a double-minded man, unstable in all he does.

The assurance we receive from knowing that nothing will ever separate us from the love of God influences the way we work. God encourages us to act on His desires by telling us that nothing pleases Him more than rewarding our faith in Him. Yes, there will be doubters who tell us that our dreams are too big, but we overcome their reservations by listening to God explain how we can't dream big enough. God points to His long history of faithfulness to keep us believing in His promises over what our eyes and naysayers tell us. He informs us that we have no need to fear the future since He's already there and knows what's going to happen, and has predetermined how to use it for our good. Knowing that God will never leave or forsake us gives us the strength to work through our issues and the fortitude to make tough decisions that carry some risk. Obviously, there will be times when our world gets rocked, but we have God's commitment that He has a firm grip on our lives and won't let go. Trusting in God's favor affects the way we labor and attracts our associates to the One whose standing right behind us.

Luke 2:11-14 Today in the town of David a Savior has been born to you; he is Christ the Lord. This will be a sign to you: "You will find a baby wrapped in cloths and lying in a manger." Suddenly a great company of the heavenly host appeared with the angel, praising God and saying, "Glory to God in the highest, and on earth peace to men on whom his favor rests."

Ephesians 3:20-21 Now to him who is able to do immeasurably more than all we ask or imagine, according to his power that is at work within us, to him be glory in the church and in Christ Jesus throughout all generations, for ever and ever! Amen.

Revelation 1:8 "I am the Alpha and the Omega," says the Lord God, "who is, and who was, and who is to come, the Almighty."

Hebrews 13:5 Keep your lives free from the love of money and be content with what you have, because God has said, "Never will I leave you; never will I forsake you."

Colossians 1:17 He is before all things, and in him all things hold together.

Psalms 36:3-6 Trust in the LORD and do good; dwell in the land and enjoy safe pasture. Delight yourself in the LORD and he will give you the desires of your heart. Commit your way to the LORD; trust in him and he will do this: He will make your righteousness shine like the dawn, the justice of your cause like the noonday sun.

Questions for Reflection

1. God tells us that faith is being sure of what we hope for and certain of what we do not see. (Hebrews 11:1) How do you incorporate your faith and hope in God into doing your job?
Examples:
   - By faith I do my job and trust that God will bless my labor.
   - I trust that God is for me and act on the desires He's puts on my heart.
   - I play it safe. Acting by faith is hard because I have failed when I have taken chances in the past.

2. What has caused you to surrender God's favor for the fear of failure? How do you get it back?
Examples:

- I didn't know I had God's favor.
- I fell into sin. I confessed and repented and let His love drive away my doubt and lead me into His favor.
- My pride only gets me so far and then I start to fear when I get over my head. I need to surrender my self-confidence for God confidence because nothing is impossible for Him.

3. Can you think of a circumstance where something didn't go the way you wanted but turned out to be good for you? Did you see God's favor in it?

Examples:
- I got laid off but ended up getting a much better job. Yes, God is amazing.
- I didn't get the promotion but heard the job turned out to be terrible. No, I never thought about how rejection could be a blessing from God.

4. Can you recollect any missed opportunities in your life that came from lack of confidence or fear of failure? Do you wish you had gone for it?

Examples:
- I didn't go out for the team because I wasn't sure I could make it.
- I never interviewed for the job because I was afraid I wouldn't get it.
- I couldn't tell the person how I felt because I didn't know if they would feel the same about me.

2

Do Great Work

We take notice of people who are great at what they do. Think back to your school days and who comes to mind? Of course we recall our close friends, but we also recollect the classmates who used their talents to do great things. I personally remember, how each of my buddies did something incredibly well. It didn't matter if it was a sport, hobby or something academic; I was amazed by their ability and passion for doing it. Seeing them gain neighborhood fame had a big influence on the clothes I wore and words I spoke. (Hang Ten, Adidas, and the word "totally") Obviously, our fascination with greatness doesn't stop in high school; it goes on for the rest of our lives. We're always going to be drawn to individuals who do wonderful things. God made us this way and it's one of the reasons why He wants us to be dedicated to doing great work. He desires to use our accomplishments to demonstrate His greatness to our colleagues. Devotion to excellence starts by believing that our Father in heaven has prepared good works for us to do on earth. If we stay diligent in using our God given skills (sometimes longer than we expected), then He rewards our faithfulness with results beyond our expectations. In a workplace filled with unbelievers, God makes Himself known through the great work we do that is done in His way.

Ephesians 2:10 For we are God's workmanship, created in Christ Jesus to do good works, which God prepared in advance for us to do.

1 Thessalonians 1:3 We continually remember before our God and Father your work produced by faith, your labor prompted by love, and your endurance inspired by hope in our Lord Jesus Christ.

Colossians 1:10-12 And we pray this in order that you may live a life worthy of the Lord and may please him in every way: bearing fruit in every good work, growing in the knowledge of God, being strengthened with all power according to his glorious might so that you may have great endurance and patience, and joyfully giving thanks to the Father, who has qualified you to share in the inheritance of the saints in the kingdom of light.

We can see the affect that greatness has on influencing people by the use of branding in the marketplace. Companies are willing to pay millions of dollars for successful athletes or celebrities to endorse their products. These public influencers may not be qualified to give an expert opinion, but it doesn't matter because their greatness in what they do draws us to listen to them. Does Michael Jordan really know the science behind sports drinks, or Roger Federer an expert in champagne? I don't know, maybe, but companies pay them for their brand and not their expertise. Marketers understand that if we admire a person's talents, then we'll most likely try the products they tell us they like. Branding is powerful and it's why the greatest athletes make more money off of their endorsements than the sport in which they excel. Understanding branding helps us see the affect that our great work has on our coworkers, family, and friends. Obviously, most of us won't be as famous as Michael Jordan, but we don't need to be to influence people for Christ. If our faith in God is seen in the deeds of our work, then our coworkers will be drawn to Him by what He does through us.

Matthew 5:14-16 "You are the light of the world. A city on a hill cannot be hidden. Neither do people light a lamp and put it under a bowl. Instead they put it on its stand, and it gives light to everyone in the house. In the same way, let your light shine before men, that they may see your good deeds and praise your Father in heaven."

<u>2 Timothy 1:7</u> For God did not give us a spirit of timidity, but a spirit of power, of love and of self-discipline.

<u>Proverbs 31:10-31</u> A wife of noble character who can find? She is worth far more than rubies. Her husband has full confidence in her and lacks nothing of value. She brings him good, not harm, all the days of her life. She selects wool and flax and works with eager hands. She is like the merchant ships, bringing her food from afar. She gets up while it is still dark; she provides food for her family and portions for her servant girls. She considers a field and buys it; out of her earnings she plants a vineyard. She sets about her work vigorously; her arms are strong for her tasks. She sees that her trading is profitable, and her lamp does not go out at night. In her hand she holds the distaff and grasps the spindle with her fingers. She opens her arms to the poor and extends her hands to the needy. When it snows, she has no fear for her household; for all of them are clothed in scarlet. She makes coverings for her bed; she is clothed in fine linen and purple. Her husband is respected at the city gate, where he takes his seat among the elders of the land. She makes linen garments and sells them, and supplies the merchants with sashes. She is clothed with strength and dignity; she can laugh at the days to come. She speaks with wisdom, and faithful instruction is on her tongue. She watches over the affairs of her household and does not eat the bread of idleness. Her children arise and call her blessed; her husband also, and he praises her: "Many women do noble things, but you surpass them all." Charm is deceptive, and beauty is fleeting; but a woman who fears the LORD is to be praised. Give her the reward she has earned, and let her works bring her praise at the city gate.

God has made us to do great things, and He cares about the way we go about accomplishing them. God's way to greatness comes by working through the power of His Spirit, rather than driven by the desires of our flesh. The endeavors that will earn us treasure in heaven are guided by God's wisdom and funded by our trust in His provision. Pride, fear, and greed can hijack the faith needed for divine success and steal the praise deserved for God. We overcome these adversaries by seeking to please the One who makes us great, rather than desiring the recognition and riches that greatness can bring. God keeps us from opening up Pandora's box to obtain our success by letting us know He's always watching and willing to help. His oversight directs us to be accountable to our coworkers so that they can see His diligence and integrity displayed in us. Unlike a financial analyst, God measures our achievements by the extent that our actions please Him and not by the amount of money our labor makes us. If we work in ways that please and exemplify God, then our accomplishments will grow His fame on earth and reward us in heaven. The more we rely on God in doing our jobs, the better we'll represent His brand in the marketplace.

> Zechariah 4:6 So he said to me, "This is the word of the LORD to Zerubbabel: 'Not by might nor by power, but by my Spirit,' says the LORD Almighty."

> 2 Chronicles 9:5-8 She (Queen of Sheba) said to the king, "The report I heard in my own country about your achievements and your wisdom is true. But I did not believe what they said until I came and saw with my own eyes. Indeed, not even half the greatness of your wisdom was told me; you have far exceeded the report I heard. How happy your men must be! How happy your officials, who continually stand before you and hear your wisdom! Praise be to the LORD your God, who has delighted in you and placed you on his throne as king to rule for the LORD your God. Because of the love of your God for Israel and his desire to uphold them for ever, he has made you king over them, to maintain justice and righteousness."

Questions for Reflection

1. What is something you are great at doing?
Examples:
   - Writing, dancing, organizing, accounting, selling, painting, public speaking

2. Are you able to use this skill in you current job? If not, why aren't you looking for work where you can utilize your talent?

Examples:

- Yes, everyday.
- No and I feel stuck in my job.
- No and I'm not sure how I can make money from my skill or talent.

3. How can you be godly great in a job that isn't so great? (Discuss ways you could add value to your duties.)

Examples:

- I can't! I hate my job.
- I can by having a good attitude and taking initiative to increase my responsibilities.
- I can by being consistently good everyday, while learning new aspects about my job.

4. What is stopping you from doing great work? Have you asked God to help you overcome it?

Examples:

- I lack a needed skill. I'm not sure why I haven't asked my boss or God to help me attain it.
- I'm in a lazy phase right now. Not motivated. I need to be encouraged by God.
- Other people are just better than me, but I'm not sure why that stops me from being the best I can be. I need to look to please God in my work rather than compete with my teammates.

3

Respect Your Boss

I've had both good and bad bosses over the last four decades. Usually, my respect for them depended on how they acted towards me and my eye for an eye attitude led to less success at work and sabotaged my happiness at home. Repeatedly, I ignored God's clear instruction to respect authority and allowed my emotions to determine my course of action. When my anger took over, it directed my subjective critical nature to seek out the specks of wrong in my managers' eyes but to overlook the plank of disobedience stuck in my own eye. Unaware of my blind spot, I kept judging my bosses even though my own resume was filled with many examples of questionable ungodly moments. Thankfully, God loves people in spite of our behavior and He indwells us to do the same. His love empowers us to treat people the same way He treats us with all of our imperfections. Over the years, God has used my frustration with my very human bosses to motivate me to rely on His Spirit instead of my flesh. I can attest that my less than stellar managers have been best at revealing the sin nature still living in me. I know it's hard to be under incompetent or arrogant leadership and you may be thinking, "Rob you haven't met my manager! He or she lies, demeans, and is immoral. There is no way I can respect them." I can only reply that even though I don't know your boss, I do know that if God commands us to respect them, then He'll empower us to obey Him.

1 Peter 2:17-21 Show proper respect to everyone: Love the brotherhood of believers, fear God, honor the king. Slaves, submit yourselves to your masters with all respect, not only to those who are good and considerate, but also to those who are harsh. For it is commendable if a man bears up under the pain of unjust suffering because he is conscious of God. But how is it to your credit if you receive a beating for doing wrong and endure it? But if you suffer for doing good and you endure it, this is commendable before God. To this you were called, because Christ suffered for you, leaving you an example, that you should follow in his steps.

Luke 6:41-42 "Why do you look at the speck of sawdust in your brother's eye and pay no attention to the plank in your own eye? How can you say to your brother, 'Brother, let me take the speck out of your eye,' when you yourself fail to see the plank in your own eye? You hypocrite, first take the plank out of your eye, and then you will see clearly to remove the speck from your brother's eye.

2 Peter 1:4 Through these he has given us his very great and precious promises, so that through them you may participate in the divine nature and escape the corruption in the world caused by evil desires.

Jude 1:8-9 In the very same way, these dreamers pollute their own bodies, reject authority and slander celestial beings. But even the archangel Michael, when he was disputing with the devil about the body of Moses, did not dare to bring a slanderous accusation against him, but said, "The Lord rebuke you!"

We all desire to have the perfect boss to mentor us, but we don't always get Jesus for a manager. It's hard to respect a supervisor who's dishonest, immoral, and easily angered; or the boss who says one thing and does another while setting unrealistic expectations. God understands, but He wants us to see the hypocrisy of responding to our manager's disrespectful behavior with a lack of respect for them. How does God expect us to revere someone who does things that the bible tells us not to do? God doesn't want us to esteem our boss's poor conduct, but rather His authority to put them in charge. We overcome our desire to demean an incompetent supervisor by fixing our thoughts on the ways of Jesus, instead of focusing on the character flaws of our manager. God's nature always demands our respect, whether our boss's actions do or not. His Spirit reminds us that God's grace is a two-sided coin: it's not earned when we receive it, so it's not deserved when we give it. If were making our manager work for our respect, then we're no longer enjoying God's grace for ourselves. Relying on our perfect God is what stops us from disrespecting our fallible boss. The more we dwell in the unconditional grace of God, the less contempt we'll have for those in authority over us.

1 Peter 2:13-15 Submit yourselves for the Lord's sake to every authority instituted among men: whether to the king, as the supreme authority, or to governors, who are sent by him to punish those who do wrong and to commend those who do right. For it is God's will that by doing good you should silence the ignorant talk of foolish men.

2 Corinthians 9:8 And God is able to make all grace abound to you, so that in all things at all times, having all that you need, you will abound in every good work.

Ephesians 3:16-21 I pray that out of his glorious riches he may strengthen you with power through his Spirit in your inner being, so that Christ may dwell in your hearts through faith. And I pray that you, being rooted and established in love, may have power, together with all the saints, to grasp how wide and long and high and deep is the love of Christ, and to know this love that surpasses knowledge--that you may be filled to the measure of all the fullness of God. Now to him who is able to do immeasurably more than all we ask or imagine, according to his power that is at work within us, to him be glory in the church and in Christ Jesus throughout all generations, for ever and ever! Amen.

Psalms 103:10 He (God) does not treat us as our sins deserve or repay us according to our iniquities.

Romans 2:4 Or do you show contempt for the riches of his kindness, tolerance and patience, not realizing that God's kindness leads you towards repentance?

Why is it that we can ignore God's voice in the anger we have for our manager, but clearly hear Him warn us of danger when stricken with fear? Yes, God uses our emotions to communicate with us and our irritation with our boss is His way of summoning us to spend some time with Him. If we answer His call, Jesus reassures us that everyone will be held responsible for his or her actions so we can stop judging. He reminds us that He overcame the sins of the world by submitting to the will of His Father, and then asks why we don't honor God in dealing with the issues of only one boss? After giving us a moment to think about our answer, Jesus redirects our eyes to see the absence of nail scars on our hands to loosen their grip on our manager's wrongdoings. He points out that in accepting His forgiveness for our sins we also agreed with His pardon of everyone else's wrongs too. How great is our God? His grace for our transgressions is forever bundled with the mercy we need to forgive those who sin against us, which leaves us with no reasons not to respect our boss. God's way of giving us a better manager in the future is by telling us to respect them just the way they are today.

1 Timothy 2:1-4 I urge, then, first of all, that requests, prayers, intercession and thanksgiving be made for everyone--for kings and all those in authority, that we may live peaceful and quiet lives in all godliness and holiness. This is good, and pleases God our Savior, who wants all men to be saved and to come to a knowledge of the truth.

Luke 6:37 "Do not judge, and you will not be judged. Do not condemn, and you will not be condemned. Forgive, and you will be forgiven."

Note: If a manager has gone beyond their authority by breaking the law then we should use the authority God has given us to bring them to justice and hopefully repentance.

Questions for Reflection
Questions for Reflection

1. Do you have the perfect boss at work? Are you a perfect employee? Do you still want to be respected?
    Examples:
    - No/No/Yes - I want to be respected.
    - No/Yes – I might want to ask others if I'm the perfect employee.

2. How do you respond when your boss acts ungodly towards you? Unknowingly is your behavior determined by their actions?
    Examples:
    - Yes, sometimes the way I'm treated affects my response.
    - No, I ignore them.
    - No, I don't like to be controlled by people. I try to treat them like God treats me.

3. Frustration with your boss could be God's way of telling you that He's at work in your life. Do you ever ask God if He's using your boss to make changes in you?
    Examples:
    - No, I don't need to change.
    - No, I've never thought the issue could be with me.
    - Yes, I know that some of my frustration comes from my insecurity in my own skills and abilities.

4. What keeps you from sharing the grace you've been given from God with your boss? How does not giving grace affect you?
    Examples:
    - My frustration with their actions. I stay frustrated.
    - I think they should earn my respect. I'm never at rest but always striving.
    - I can't give people what they don't deserve. I live feeling judged and unsettled.

4

Be Honest and Trustworthy

We all like to work with trustworthy people. Yet, the workplace is filled with folks who flat out lie and others who think that half the truth is good enough. We can't escape working with associates who try to further their careers with misleading statements or timely amnesia. It's in hearing a salesperson stretch the truth to close the sale that we observe how motive can distort reality. Greed in the marketplace has a way of turning normally black and white thinking people into greys. Working with folks who have no intention of fulfilling their commitments causes us both frustration and harm. Corruption, bribery, and fraud painfully teach us that character and integrity matter. The hurtful lies that negatively affect our lives can turn each of us into a doubting Thomas. The older we get the more we can think we'll never find someone who's honest and trustworthy. God knows what were seeking and wants us to find the truth we're looking for in His Son. Jesus is the way and the truth and the life, and our faith in Him will transform us to be honest too. Taking God up on any of His promises will give us first hand experience to how faithful He is to fulfilling them. There are many ways God uses us to lead our coworkers to Christ, but none are more important than trustworthy actions and words that are true.

John 14:6 Jesus answered, "I am the way and the truth and the life. No-one comes to the Father except through me."

Luke 16:10 "Whoever can be trusted with very little can also be trusted with much, and whoever is dishonest with very little will also be dishonest with much."

Satan is the father of lies, which means he's not only a good liar, but also cunningly adept at motivating us to lie too. He subtly deceives us into speaking little fibs today to lead us into telling bigger lies tomorrow. Shrewdly, Satan tries to make us believe that some lies are ok by telling us that nobody's going to find out or get hurt by them. Yet in reality, God always knows if we lie and saddened when we do; heartbroken that we've been deceived into believing that He doesn't always love us, and that His promises aren't true. So, if we're in the habit of lying, then it makes sense for God to go out of His way to express His love for us. God uses discipline with internal guilt and external circumstances to motivate us to come to Him with our sin. His unfailing love leads us into confessing and repenting of the untruths that we've told to make us right again. God nips our problem in the bud because he doesn't want our coworkers, family, and friends having trouble trusting in Him because of the lies coming out of us. Yes, God hates lying lips, but He loves liars and this truth sets us free from being deceived into telling more lies.

John 8:31-32 To the Jews who had believed him, Jesus said, "If you hold to my teaching, you are really my disciples. Then you will know the truth, and the truth will set you free."

Hebrews 12:6 because the Lord disciplines those he loves, and he punishes everyone he accepts as a son."

Luke 22:60-62 Peter replied, "Man, I don't know what you're talking about!" Just as he was speaking, the cock crowed. The Lord turned and looked straight at Peter. Then Peter remembered the word the Lord had spoken to him: "Before the cock crows today, you will disown me three times." And he went outside and wept bitterly.

Ephesians 4:25 Therefore each of you must put off falsehood and speak truthfully to his neighbor, for we are all members of one body.

Psalms 145:13 Your kingdom is an everlasting kingdom, and your dominion endures through all generations. The LORD is faithful to all his promises and loving towards all he has made.

What goes along with honesty is being trustworthy. We acquire this quality by worshiping the faithfulness of God in our life. It's our belief in God's unfailing love that gives us a heart that is faithful and true. God knows that our ability to keep our commitments is contingent upon how much we rely on Him to help fulfill them. The greater we trust in God, the more authority His Spirit has to live out His character in us. The loyalty that God has shown us in the past is meant to grow our dependence on His Word today. Obeying God in all the things we do at work allows our coworkers to see that they can trust us and depend on Him too. If our coworkers are going to experience Jesus living in us, then what we say needs to be what we do. Every time we keep our word and meet a deadline we display God's nature to our teammates. Our ability to keep confidences and not condemn our coworkers leads them to trust that Jesus Christ really did come into the world to save sinners. An honest days work earns us more than a paycheck when the way we labor helps our coworkers to believe in God.

James 1:22 Do not merely listen to the word, and so deceive yourselves. Do what it says.

Proverbs 11:13 A gossip betrays a confidence, but a trustworthy man keeps a secret.

1 Timothy 1:15 Here is a trustworthy saying that deserves full acceptance: Christ Jesus came into the world to save sinners--of whom I am the worst.

John 4:23 Yet a time is coming and has now come when the true worshippers will worship the Father in spirit and truth, for they are the kind of worshippers the Father seeks.

Titus 2:9-10 Teach slaves to be subject to their masters in everything, to try to please them, not to talk back to them, and not to steal from them, but to show that they can be fully trusted, so that in every way they will make the teaching about God our Savior attractive.

Questions for Reflection

1. What makes you lie?
Examples:
   - I don't want to hurt somebody's feelings.
   - I don't want to get in trouble.
   - I want something and I need to lie to get it.
   - I'm not sure – I just got in the habit of telling little white lies.
   - I don't lie – which might be a lie.

2. How do you feel when you find out that you have been lied to? How does God feel when we lie?
Examples:
   - I feel betrayed. God has compassion for the person I've lied to.
   - I lose trust in that person. God is sad because we don't trust Him.
   - I am angry. God hates lying.

3. What are things you can do at work that will help your coworkers to trust you? Do you do them? Why not?
Examples:
   - Show up on time.
   - Keep our commitments.
   - Tell the truth, even when we mess up.

4. How does lying affect your relationships and your testimony?
Examples:
   - Relationships suffer because of trust issues.
   - People find it hard to believe what I say, which would include my testimony.
   - People see no difference in me to others, and think that I'm just another hypocritical Christian.

5

Pray Instead of Complain

I once had a boss who made it pretty easy for those of us on his team to complain about all the things he did or didn't do. For at least a year, I routinely found myself, and my peers taking turns criticizing our manager as if we were playing a game of Ping-Pong. One prayerful morning when I was complaining to the Lord about my manager's lying, manipulating, and cunning ability to take credit for work done by others, I finally heard a response from Him. God said to me, "I know all about your manager, why don't you tell me the qualities you'd like in a boss? I thought to myself, "Finally, God has heard my prayer!" Then I described my perfect manager, "I'd like someone who was honest, straightforward, kind, and humble. I paused for a moment to think of more godly attributes, when God stated, "It sounds like you want a Christian manager?" I excitedly said, "Yes, that's exactly what I want!" I started to praise God for his insight, when He asked me yet another question, "If you want a godly manager, then why haven't you prayed for your current boss to be saved?" Sadly, I had no answer and realized that my constant complaining had kept me from praying for the salvation of those in authority over me.

1 Timothy 2:1-4 I urge, then, first of all, that requests, prayers, intercession and thanksgiving be made for everyone--for kings and all those in authority, that we may live peaceful and quiet lives in all godliness and holiness. This is good, and pleases God

our Savior, who wants all men to be saved and to come to a knowledge of the truth.

<u>Philippians 2:14-16</u> Do everything without complaining or arguing, so that you may become blameless and pure, children of God without fault in a crooked and depraved generation, in which you shine like stars in the universe as you hold out the word of life—in order that I may boast on the day of Christ that I did not run or labor for nothing.

<u>Mark 2:17</u> On hearing this, Jesus said to them, "It is not the healthy who need a doctor, but the sick. I have not come to call the righteous, but sinners."

What's more frustrating than a difficult person in the office? When the copier or printer stops working! Nobody likes a broken photocopier except a Xerox sales representative. I should know because I used to be one. Don't take this wrong, but I loved it when a copier broke down because this workplace issue was an opportunity for me to sell a new one. It doesn't take long in life to learn that our vantage point of a situation affects the way we see and respond to it. When it comes to encountering difficult people, God wants us to view them from His heavenly perspective. Observing our coworkers through Spirit filled eyes allows us to see their ungodly actions as signs of need, rather than as reasons to complain. If we knew what God knows about our fellow associates, it would change the way we think about them. God has seen all of their emotional trauma, physical pain, and soulful guilt, and He wants us to share His compassion for the beating life's given them. It's in considering the circumstances behind a person's behavior that moves our lips to pray, rather than complain. The divine empathy we need to love on a rude coworker comes by asking God to show us how patient He's been with us over the years. Praying to the One who's extremely attentive to fulfilling our needs will give us the grace required to lead a self-centered person to Jesus. Although God doesn't always let us choose our coworkers, He does always give us the choice to how we will respond to their inconsiderate actions. Yes, yelling can seem to release our anger for the moment, but it never transforms the other person; it only changes us for the worse. Griping always hardens our heart and prompts us to complain more and more. Ironically, when we're complaining about the actions of others, Jesus is praying for a change in us.

Philippians 4:6-7 Do not be anxious about anything, but in everything, by prayer and petition, with thanksgiving, present your requests to God. And the peace of God, which transcends all understanding, will guard your hearts and your minds in Christ Jesus.

Matthew 5:44-46 But I tell you: Love your enemies and pray for those who persecute you, that you may be sons of your Father in heaven. He causes his sun to rise on the evil and the good, and sends rain on the righteous and the unrighteous. If you love those who love you, what reward will you get? Are not even the tax collectors doing that?

We illuminate God's light by the good things we do, but we also light up our workplace by what we don't do: not complaining even though we have good reasons to protest. God sets us up to shine by putting us in difficult situations at work, but unfortunately we can miss our opportunity by complaining about the darkness He put us into light. Too many times, I've been guilty of voicing my frustrations to associates rather than praying them to God. I've learned the hard way that complaining never brings the satisfaction we long for; but it's good at turning our anger into bitterness. When our self-concern is greater than our trust in God we will whine about our colleagues, rather than pray for Jesus to intervene. I've missed many promptings to pray for my coworkers because my priority was on getting my needs met, rather than God's will done. Even when I did pray, most times I petitioned for God's vengeance to come upon my workplace foes, instead of His longsuffering Spirit to touch my heart. After many years of frustration, I've learned that complaining about my colleagues is a sign of unresolved sin in me. God knows we won't dwell on the faults of others after we've been freed from the shame of our sins.

John 8:36 So if the Son sets you free, you will be free indeed.

Matthew 6:12 Forgive us our debts, as we also have forgiven our debtors.

Matthew 9:10-13 While Jesus was having dinner at Matthew's house, many tax collectors and "sinners" came and ate with him and his disciples. When the Pharisees saw this, they asked his disciples, "Why does your teacher eat with tax collectors and 'sinners'?" On hearing this, Jesus said, "It is not the healthy who need a doctor, but the sick. But go and learn what this means: 'I desire mercy, not sacrifice.' For I have not come to call the righteous, but sinners."

1 Peter 2:22-24 "He committed no sin, and no deceit was found in his mouth." When they hurled their insults at him, he did not retaliate; when he suffered, he made no threats. Instead, he entrusted himself to him who judges justly. He himself bore our sins in his body on the tree, so that we might die to sins and live for righteousness; by his wounds you have been healed.

Praying doesn't mean we don't do anything when we've been wronged at work, but we first seek God's direction and restoration. God knows that complaining comes with feelings of hopelessness so He reminds us that He's bigger than any workplace bully. Petitioning God gives us hope and moves our eyes to look for His good in the situation, rather than focusing on the wrongs of our coworkers. If we trust God to deal with the sins of others, then He will help us overcome our emotions so we can navigate through our conflicts in righteousness. Pleading with Jesus restrains us from doing evil and tames our tongue so that we speak the truth in love and don't say words we'll regret later. Praying downloads the grace required to forgive our coworkers, even before they ask to be. Talking to God stops us from yelling at people, and our silence proclaims our faith in a Savior who didn't retaliate against those who hung His body on a tree. Every day, the wrongs of others give us a reason to speak to God and the opportunity to share the gospel with our coworkers by the words we don't say.

1 Peter 3:12-17 For the eyes of the Lord are on the righteous and his ears are attentive to their prayer, but the face of the Lord is against those who do evil." Who is going to harm you if you are eager to do good? But even if you should suffer for what is right, you are blessed. "Do not fear what they fear; do not be

frightened." But in your hearts set apart Christ as Lord. Always be prepared to give an answer to everyone who asks you to give the reason for the hope that you have. But do this with gentleness and respect, keeping a clear conscience, so that those who speak maliciously against your good behavior in Christ may be ashamed of their slander. It is better, if it is God's will, to suffer for doing good than for doing evil.

Romans 8:28 And we know that in all things God works for the good of those who love him, who have been called according to his purpose.

There are times when our frustration with our manager is a sign that God is at work in our life, and not theirs. God has no problem using a demanding boss to move us out of our comfort zone to grow our faith in Him and His character in us. If God is behind the changes that we're being asked to do, then we should stop protesting so He can start renovating the way we work. This makes perfect sense when talking about someone else, but can be overwhelming when we're the ones being asked to learn a new skill. It doesn't take long for our self-doubt to get us searching for other disgruntled employees to collaborate with and justify our non-compliance. Ironically, it's our own griping that does more damage to our job satisfaction than the changes our manager is asking us to do. Reminiscing about the good old days gets us complaining about bad new days and we miss out the blessings of God today. Unfortunately, I can testify that resisting progress only slows our growth and steals the joy that comes with seeing God work in our lives. Praying to God instead of complaining to our coworkers is how we overcome our fear and embrace what's new and unknown. It's by welcoming change rather than fighting it, that we lead our hesitant coworkers into trusting God too.

Ecclesiastes 7:10 (NLT) 10 Don't long for "the good old days," for you don't know whether they were any better than today.

2 Thessalonians 1:11-12 With this in mind, we constantly pray for you, that our God may count you worthy of his calling, and that by his power he may fulfill every good purpose of yours and

every act prompted by your faith. We pray this so that the name of our Lord Jesus may be glorified in you, and you in him, according to the grace of our God and the Lord Jesus Christ.

<u>1 Peter 2:13-14</u> Submit yourselves for the Lord's sake to every authority instituted among men: whether to the king, as the supreme authority, or to governors, who are sent by him to punish those who do wrong and to commend those who do right.

Note – If you're in a management position, God wants you to work hard to do business His way and resolve injustices. God will give you the courage and integrity you need through His Word and in prayer. If you're an employee, you should do your part by letting management know of any practices that don't represent the values stated by the company. (Not complaining but by being forthright) Also, if a violation has occurred, you should go to your manager, human resources, or law enforcement official to use the means God has given to bring you justice. Whether we're in management or not, God always wants us to come to the aid of others being wronged.

Questions for Reflection

1. Why does complaining make things worse instead of better?
Examples:
   - Complaining about work brings negativity into my home.
   - It makes me look petty and hurts my career.
   - It doesn't make things worse, it makes me feel better to blow off steam and it gets people working harder.
   - It negatively affects the lives of the people who have to listen to me.

2. Who is the one person you should vent our frustration? Why?
Examples:
   - My wife or husband because they have to listen to me.
   - Jesus because He's willing to listen and can provide what I need.
   - My boss because they should know everything that is going on.

3. Do you see the sinful actions of others as signs of their need or reasons to complain?

Examples:

- Signs of their need – I once was complaining about someone and found out their spouse had been diagnosed with cancer. I felt terrible!
- Reasons to complain – Their actions affect me.
- Both – I complain and pray – I complain about people and then I pray for God to do something.

4. What happens when you pray for coworkers?

Examples:

- We bring the power God into our circumstances.
- We give the sin of our colleagues to the One who will judge righteously, so we don't become judgmental.
- We get to enjoy our lives and not be held hostage by the actions of others.

6

Get to Know New People

We naturally gravitate to people we like, know, or who are similar to us. I understand this all too well from the customer dinners I hosted over the years. At many of these events, I would look around and see that most of our team, including myself, was sitting together rather than spread out amongst the partners; the ones we had invited to get to know better! It was more relaxing to eat dinner with people we already knew and liked, instead of dealing with the anxiety of striking up a conversation with someone new and unknown. God knows it's easier for us to spend time with those who share our faith in Jesus; nevertheless, He calls and empowers us to also befriend people who don't know Him. If we take a genuine interest in the lives of our coworkers, then we'll get chances to share with them the life of God who lives in us. Obviously, it's not easy to meet new people but God is more than willing to help us with the introductions. Jesus went out of His way to make friends and He wants us to do the same because friendships allow us to share His love in a way that only a friend can do.

> 1 Corinthians 5:9-11 I have written to you in my letter not to associate with sexually immoral people--not at all meaning the people of this world who are immoral, or the greedy and swindlers, or idolaters. In that case you would have to leave this world. But now I am writing to you that you must not associate with anyone who calls himself a brother but is sexually immoral or

greedy, an idolater or a slanderer, a drunkard or a swindler. With such a man do not even eat.

Romans 12:15-16 Rejoice with those who rejoice; mourn with those who mourn. Live in harmony with one another. Do not be proud, but be willing to associate with people of low position. Do not be conceited.

Work brings people from different backgrounds, beliefs, and cultures together. We don't have to go half way around the world to be on a mission's trip, we simply need to go to work wanting to get to know our associates. We can think that being intentional to meet someone doesn't have a big affect, but it does. If we reflect on the friends we have today, then we know how one caring gesture can turn complete strangers into life long buddies. We all enjoy spending time with good friends, but God encourages us to keep making new acquaintances so that more people can get to know Him by getting to know us. If insecurity is keeping us from reaching out to our coworkers, then we need to take some time to understand how valuable we are to God. Drawing close to God allows His love to overwhelm our anxiety. The strength of His presence gives us the courage to befriend the people He's put in our lives. The more we accept that we're loved and adored by God, the less we'll worry about what everybody else thinks about us.

John 15:15 I no longer call you servants, because a servant does not know his master's business. Instead, I have called you friends, for everything that I learned from my Father I have made known to you.

1 Peter 5:7 Cast all your anxiety on him because he cares for you.

Most of us spend more waking hours Monday through Friday at work, than we do at home. The time we spend with our coworkers and the work we do together helps us make new friendships. Every day in our jobs, we endure trials and celebrate successes with our teammates. Through business cycles and seasons of life, both laughter and heartbreak bonds us with our cubicle mates. We endure the uncertainty of layoffs and reorgs by praying for our coworkers and taking time to console each other. We spend lunchtimes discussing which medical plan, 401K-investment option, and next job we should pursue. Together, we go on diets, start exercise programs, and help one another fight against all the things that declare war on our health. At the end of the day, we walk to our cars pondering the schools our kids should attend and mutually wondering how we're going to pay for college. We come back from vacations and share our photos and stories of the special times in our life. Years go by and we get to know each other's families as we watch our infants grow up to be college students. The workplace is perfect for meeting new people and God goes out the way to give us an environment to help us make friends. Why? It's simple. Friends of God, share God with their friends. We need to realize that people can't hear our testimony if we never talk to them. Most of the time, sharing God's love starts by saying, "Hi, my name is Rob, what's yours?"

> <u>1 Thessalonian 3:12</u> May the Lord make your love increase and overflow for each other and for everyone else, just as ours does for you.

Note: We must be sensitive to the leading of God's Spirit as we interact with new people. God may direct us to stay away from a person to guard us from being hurt or negatively influenced by them. God knows whose heart's can be touched by us, and when our words will fall on deaf ears. God will show us the coworkers we should keep at a safe distance and of those to invest in. We must follow His lead and be praying for direction on whom to befriend at work.

Questions for Reflection

1. Who's your best friend at work? How did you become friends? Do you have any non-Christian friends?

Examples:
   - Rob, we became friends over time by the interactions in our job.
   - Yes, I have non-Christian friends.

2. What stops you from meeting new people at work?

Examples:
- I'm too busy.
- I'm not an outgoing person.
- It's work. I have my own circle of friends outside of the workplace.

3. Would your job be more enjoyable if you worked with friends?
Examples:
- Yes, friends would be more helpful and kind.
- Yes, it would be nice to be around friends at work.
- No, I don't need the drama that comes with having more friends.

4. Do your friends at work know about your faith in God? Is it by your actions or did you get a chance to share your testimony?
Examples:
- Yes, they saw me reading the bible at lunch and asked me about it.
- No, I don't think it's any of their business.
- I'm not sure.
- Yes, they were going through a trial and I asked if I could pray for them. This prayer lead to an opportunity to share my faith in Jesus.

7

Forgive and Do Good When Wronged

We notice things that are wonderful and different. It's the wow factor of a new style, design, or technology that stops us in our tracks and makes our heads turn. God understands how something amazing can make us pause and take notice. It's why He creates incredible sunsets, beautiful smiles, and newborn babies. It's also why He supplies us with unending grace to share with the people we work with every day. Nothing drops jaws more at work than when we treat people better than their actions deserve. Responding to a wrong by doing something right lights up the darkness of a "dog-eat-dog" workplace. We teach our coworkers about the mercy of God by forgiving their offences that if done by us would bring their condemnation. God's voice is heard in the office when we say something nice to the coworker who's been saying mean things behind our backs. It's easy for us to get caught up in career competition, but if we see our coworkers as rivals, then we'll look to harm rather than bless them. God refrains us from returning evil with evil by letting us know that no one can stop Him from fulfilling the plans He has for our life. We stay in God's love and make His love known by letting His mercy and grace dictate our responses instead of our disdain.

> Luke 6:31-35 Do to others as you would have them do to you. "If you love those who love you, what credit is that to you? Even 'sinners' love those who love them. And if you do good to those who are good to you, what credit is that to you? Even 'sinners' do

that. And if you lend to those from whom you expect repayment, what credit is that to you? Even 'sinners' lend to 'sinners', expecting to be repaid in full. But love your enemies, do good to them, and lend to them without expecting to get anything back. Then your reward will be great, and you will be sons of the Most High, because he is kind to the ungrateful and wicked.

Colossians 3:13 Bear with each other and forgive whatever grievances you may have against one another. Forgive as the Lord forgave you.

Matthew 7:1-2 "Do not judge, or you too will be judged. For in the same way as you judge others, you will be judged, and with the measure you use, it will be measured to you."

Successful people in business and investing take advantage of the openings they see in the market. They have the initiative and understanding to seek out and find profitable opportunities, and the courage to commit and take action. Granted, not all of us have this ability, but God gives each of His children a heavenly perspective to see the wrongs of others as opportunities to do right. Like a seasoned stock trader who's buying when everyone else is selling, God wants our actions to be guided by His Spirit rather than our emotions. God knows we get greater returns by endowing His grace in people who do us wrong over those who treat us right. God profits when we invest in the low points of our coworkers' lives instead of waiting for them to improve. Obviously, leading with kindness doesn't mean we never discipline an employee, but we correct and instruct with gentleness and respect. It's by forgiving an associate who's expecting retaliation that we disarm them in a way no argument or mean rebuke could ever do. We serve a God who used grace to save and transform our lives and His charity desires more than only us. He wants His undeserved love of us to be shared with others so He can change their lives too.

Ephesians 2:8 For it is by grace you have been saved, through faith--and this not from yourselves, it is the gift of God—

1 Thessalonians 5:15 Make sure that nobody pays back wrong for wrong, but always try to be kind to each other and to everyone else.

It can be difficult to find the right occasion to share our faith at work, but we'll get many chances to reveal God's love through the inconsiderate actions of our coworkers. Yes, it's good to tell a teammate over a cup of coffee that Jesus loves them, but it's better to share His unconditional love by being nice to them after they've been mean to us. God wants the kindness of His ways to determine our behavior, rather than the unfriendly acts of our colleagues. Jesus points us to the cross to show us how our good God responds to bad people and reminds us that He used love to overcome the sins of the world. Surrendering our pride by forgiving a coworker and then bombing them with good deeds is God's way of ending an office war. He knows that forgiveness has divine power to lead our coworkers to Christ and bring healing to the wounds they've inflicted on us. Yes, it hurts to be insulted, but it gives us a chance to demonstrate the gospel in a way that words alone could never convey. Knowing that nothing can separate us from the love of God keeps us from pushing away our coworkers after they've done something wrong to us. Doing good is what God always does and we lead others to Jesus by doing it too.

1 Peter 3:9 Do not repay evil with evil or insult with insult, but with blessing, because to this you were called so that you may inherit a blessing.

Psalms 37:1-8 Do not fret because of evil men or be envious of those who do wrong; for like the grass they will soon wither, like green plants they will soon die away. Trust in the LORD and do good; dwell in the land and enjoy safe pasture. Delight yourself in the LORD and he will give you the desires of your heart. Commit your way to the LORD; trust in him and he will do this: He will make your righteousness shine like the dawn, the justice of your cause like the noonday sun. Be still before the LORD and wait patiently for him; do not fret when men succeed in their ways, when they carry out their wicked schemes. Refrain from anger and turn from wrath; do not fret--it leads only to evil.

Questions for Reflection
Questions for Reflection

1. Does God treat you the way your actions deserve? Give examples of God's grace in your life.
Examples:
    *   No or Yes – Any story of God's grace in your life.

2. How do you respond to self-centered people at work? What's something good you can do for them?
Examples:
    *   I don't let them push me around. If they push me hard, I push back harder.
    *   I avoid them.
    *   I think about the grace that God's given me before I respond to them.
    *   I can invite them to eat lunch with me. I can complement them on their work.

3. What stops you from sharing God's grace with those who need it most?
Examples:
    *   Not accepting or acknowledging the grace that's been given to me.
    *   I judge people. I forget that God sees what's going on and will judge perfectly, so I don't have to.
    *   If I'm grace needy, then I don't have it to give to others.

4. How do you hate the sin but love the sinner in a workplace situation? For example, if someone keeps missing deadlines and wants you to lie for them to cover it up.
Examples:
    *   I explain that I can't cover for them and tell everybody what they're doing.
    *   I lie for them because that's what I would want them to do for me.
    *   I tell them that I can't cover for them, but ask if something is wrong and how I can help.

8

Influence Rather than Adopt a Worldly Culture

God wants us to get to know our coworkers and introduce them to Him who lives in us. Fortunately, God doesn't leave us alone in our friendships and is always encouraging us to be a godly influence in the lives of our fellow workers. He knows that relationships at work aren't easy because when godliness interacts with worldliness it produces all kinds of turbulence. We live for a God who is pleased with truth, humility, and sacrifice, while the world makes truth relative and rewards greed, pleasure, and selfish ambition. These differences will test us and try to pull us away from following Jesus. We must remember that God is light and His children expose darkness rather than get overcome by it. God warns us to have nothing to do with the fruitless deeds of darkness, which will have us redirecting gossip filled conversations or abruptly leaving dinners that turn into bachelor parties. While it's true that most company's have good values in their mission statements, many have unwritten ones too. We can easily get caught up in the "do whatever it takes to get the business" mindset, or "the work hard, play hard" culture. At some companies, a rising star will be expected to participate in activities that God commands us not to do. God knows if our main desire at work is to get a promotion, then we'll be drawn away from obeying His principles and into adopting the culture of our workplace.

1 Peter 2:11-12 Dear friends, I urge you, as aliens and strangers in the world, to abstain from sinful desires, which war against your soul. Live such good lives among the pagans that, though they accuse you of doing wrong, they may see your good deeds and glorify God on the day he visits us.

Ephesians 5:8-11 For you were once darkness, but now you are light in the Lord. Live as children of light (for the fruit of the light consists in all goodness, righteousness and truth) and find out what pleases the Lord. Have nothing to do with the fruitless deeds of darkness, but rather expose them.

Proverbs 22:4 Keep away from angry, short-tempered people, or you will learn to be like them and endanger your soul.

It's very easy for us to be affected by our work environment, instead of the other way around. We all know how tricky it is to navigate friendships with people of the world without becoming worldly ourselves. I remember my mom telling me when I was young; "You will end up acting like your friends so pick them carefully!" She was right, and it's why God must always be our best friend. Jesus needs to be the friend we talk and listen to throughout the day, everyday. The divine hand we grab in times of uncertainty and the person we live to please moment-by-moment. If Jesus is our best friend, then we'll bring Him into all of our relationships whether at work or home. His Spirit will direct our conversations and guide our actions so that the way we work draws people to God. Naturally, some of our associates won't like God's influence on their business since His light exposes the darkness of their ways. They'll pressure us to leave Him out of the workplace and explain how our moral standards don't apply to them. Kindly, but firmly, we must resist because the light that makes them feel guilty also illuminates the way to God's grace and forgiveness. Yes, insults come with being a friend of Jesus, but they remind us that one day we'll be rewarded in heaven for influencing people for God on earth today.

Genesis 6:9 This is the account of Noah. Noah was a righteous man, blameless among the people of his time, and he walked with God.

<u>Matthew 5:11-12</u> "Blessed are you when people insult you, persecute you and falsely say all kinds of evil against you because of me. Rejoice and be glad, because great is your reward in heaven, for in the same way they persecuted the prophets who were before you.

<u>James 3:13</u> Who is wise and understanding among you? Let him show it by his good life, by deeds done in the humility that comes from wisdom.

Great leaders have well defined values, priorities, and goals; everybody knows what's important to them. God leads this way, and we direct others to Him when our actions make it clear that Jesus is the Lord of our life. We do this by being honest, hardworking, and wise in our labor, while being respectful, forgiving, and kind to the people in our workplace. The love of God pursues our teammates each time we treat them the way we want to be treated. It's our willingness to help instead of compete with our fellow workers that makes them feel loved rather than judged. Valuing the lives of our coworkers is how they come to appreciate the life of Jesus they experience living in us. The way God changes a work culture is the same way He saves us: through love. God's love softens hearts, restores souls, and transforms lives. The best way for us to love our coworkers is by staying true to our faith, instead of acting one way at home and another way at work. The greater our transparency, the more God's love will shine through us and influence the people we interact with every day.

<u>1 Corinthians 5:12</u> What business is it of mine to judge those outside the church? Are you not to judge those inside? God will judge those outside.

<u>1 Corinthians 13:4-8a</u> Love is patient, love is kind. It does not envy, it does not boast, it is not proud. It is not rude, it is not self-seeking, it is not easily angered, it keeps no record of wrongs. Love does not delight in evil but rejoices with the truth. It always protects, always trusts, always hopes, always perseveres. Love never fails.

Questions for Reflection

1. Do your coworkers know that you're a Christian? Why or why not?
Examples:
    *   Yes or No. Explain how they know or don't know.

2. Do you act and speak differently at church than in the office? If yes, why?
Examples:
    *   Yes, I want to fit in so I act like churchgoers at church and like my associates while at work.
    *   I'm not sure. I hope not.
    *   No, I am who I am wherever I am.

3. Who is influencing whom? Are your ways having an impact on your Non-Christian work friends or is it the other way around?
Examples:
    *   I'm influencing my coworkers about the ways of God, and they are teaching me about their culture and what's important to them.
    *   I have started to be influenced by the worldly habits of my coworkers. I'm using words I shouldn't and acting more like them and less like Jesus.
    *   I kind of do my own thing. So there isn't much influence either way.

4. What person has had the biggest influence on your life? Were they true to who they said they were or wishy-washy?
Examples:
    *   My best friend growing up. He was the real deal.
    *   My high school coach, but later on I learned that he didn't practice what he taught. Very disappointing.
    *   My mom. She was always brave and loving.

9

Humbly do the Work

There are no perfect jobs. Every occupation has some duties we enjoy and others we endure. All of us will be assigned tasks that we would never volunteer to do on our own. We don't always get the choice assignment, but we can always choose to work hard at what we've been chosen to do. God calls us to be diligent and do our best regardless of whether we like what we're doing or not. He wants us to realize that our coworkers are watching and making judgments about the authenticity of our faith. Working hard when our boss is absent demonstrates our belief that God is always present and will one day judge the actions of our lives. Our lack of complaining or comparing of workloads speaks loudly in a workplace that is used to hearing the protests of employees. Yes, coworkers will take advantage of our obedience to God, but before we say this isn't right, do we have a better way to witness His grace to them? Remember, the people who exploit the fruit of our faith will also receive the seeds of our belief. By doing the work that nobody else wants to do, we make our teammates contemplate a God they've never seen, yet clearly see us serve. God knows that it's hard to be diligent on work that won't increase our paycheck; nevertheless, it's the kind of labor that He uses to grow His kingdom.

Colossians 3:23-24 Whatever you do, work at it with all your heart, as working for the Lord, not for men, since you know that you will receive an inheritance from the Lord as a reward. It is the Lord Christ you are serving.

Matthew 5:41 If someone forces you to go one mile, go with him two miles.

Ephesians 6:5-8 Slaves, obey your earthly masters with respect and fear, and with sincerity of heart, just as you would obey Christ. Obey them not only to win their favor when their eye is on you, but like slaves of Christ, doing the will of God from your heart. Serve wholeheartedly, as if you were serving the Lord, not men, because you know that the Lord will reward everyone for whatever good he does, whether he is slave or free.

The pace of change in the workplace has never been greater. It's no longer a question of if we will have to switch companies or industries in our lifetime, but only how many times? After being forced to change jobs, it can be difficult to be enthusiastic about a new assignment that comes with more work and less benefits. God understands, but wants us to stop talking behind the backs of the people who've let us down and express our concerns to Him. When we explain how far we've fallen down the company ladder, God reminds us of all that Jesus accomplished after being reassigned from heaven to earth. He goes on to tell us that in His kingdom the most prestigious job title is "servant" and that our new position gives us an opportunity for eternal greatness. Yes, it's hard to have enthusiasm for our job after we've loss confidence in management, but God uses our doubt in them to get us back to working by faith in Him. Regardless of our spot on the company org chart, if we put ourselves under God's authority, then His holy perfection will inspire us to humbly do our work.

1 Thessalonians 1:3 We continually remember before our God and Father your work produced by faith, your labor prompted by love, and your endurance inspired by hope in our Lord Jesus Christ.

Matthew 23:11 The greatest among you will be your servant.

Colossians 1:29 To this end I labor, struggling with all his energy, which so powerfully works in me.

Philippians 2:13 For it is God who works in you to will and to act according to his good purpose.

1 Thessalonians 4:11-12 Make it your ambition to lead a quiet life, to mind your own business and to work with your hands, just as we told you, so that your daily life may win the respect of outsiders and so that you will not be dependent on anybody.

Most people know the godly principle of reaping what we sow, and the hard work we do allows God to demonstrate His faithfulness to us, and our workplace. God keeps His commitments, however He doesn't always fulfill them on our schedule. God's plans may call for more sowing than we desire to do, and our impatience can tempt us to shortcut His process. I understand all too well how worldly ambition can lead us down this wrong path. Early in my career at Xerox, I wanted to make the money that more tenured salespeople were earning. I strategically plotted for ways to be promoted, rather than simply working hard each day. Frustrated and lacking direction, I went to a manager friend of mine and asked how I could fast track a promotion. He responded with a chuckle because I had only been in my job for six months, and then he gave me some advice I've never forgotten. He said, "Just do the job you were hired to do. Work hard, learn the business, and the promotion will come." This wasn't what I wanted to hear, but I left his office knowing he was right and started focusing on doing my job rather than getting promoted.

Proverbs 21:5 Good planning and hard work lead to prosperity, but hasty shortcuts lead to poverty. (NLT)

Matthew 23:11-12 The greatest among you will be your servant. For whoever exalts himself will be humbled, and whoever humbles himself will be exalted.

For the next three quarters, I worked hard and stayed attentive to doing all the little things that I had neglected to do before. Amazingly, when the year ended I was named the top sales representative on our team. During the award's dinner, my boss pulled me aside to tell me that I would be getting a promotion and I couldn't stop smiling because my friend had been right. Then, my manager thanked me for my hard work and immediately the principle of reaping what we sow came to my mind. Incredibly, my workplace experience triggered a Sunday school memory and implanted a seed of faith in my heart that God could be trusted. Six years later, the seed grew into salvation when I gave my life to the Lord. I would go on to learn that I wasn't the only one God was working on that year at Xerox. A decade after selling my last copier, I received a card from a friend of mine on that sales team. In her note, she told me that she was now a born again Christian and said she wasn't surprised to hear that I had become a child of God too. I could only smile in thinking about how God can change lives through our seemingly insignificant labor.

2 Corinthians 9:6 Remember this: Whoever sows sparingly will also reap sparingly, and whoever sows generously will also reap generously.

John 6:29 Jesus answered, "The work of God is this: to believe in the one he has sent."

Galatians 6:9 Let us not become weary in doing good, for at the proper time we will reap a harvest if we do not give up.

Questions for Reflection

1. Name something you love doing in you job and then something you don't like to do?
Examples:
   - I love being creative. I hate doing expense reports.
   - I love big projects. I hate spreadsheets.
   - I love working with certain people. I hate team meetings.

2. Do you put forth the same effort on tasks you like and dislike? Why or why not?
Examples:

- No. Why would I?
- I try to because I don't want to get fired.
- Yes. I work hard on the tasks I don't like to do so I can get them done quickly.

3. Think of something that you didn't like to do in a job that actually turned into something that you like doing now or has helped grow your career.

Examples:

- A forecasting spreadsheet – I hated doing it at first, but grew to depend on it.
- I hated speaking in front of groups and now I love doing it.
- I hated doing budgets, but now realize it's important to the success of any project.

4. Has your work ethic been affected by focusing on the negative parts of your job? Why is it so easy to focus on the negative over the positive?

Examples:

- Yes, I dread going in on Fridays because of a long boring meeting.
- Yes, I don't like dealing with this one person.
- No, I try to focus on the positive.
- I'm not sure why the negative takes over my focus. In general, people complain more about what they don't like, than complement what they do like.

10

Give God Glory and Credit to Others in Our Success

Whether we know it or not, God's handiwork is involved in everything we achieve. Why does God go out of His way to help make us successful? God wants to use the great things He accomplishes through us to make ourselves and our coworkers stand in awe of Him. I personally learned this myself while working at Apple; let me explain. It was during the period when it looked like Apple was going out of business and Steve Jobs was returning to the company that he founded. Sales were in a sharp decline, layoffs seemed to be happening each week, and everyone was worried about losing their jobs. At the time, I was managing Apple's largest partner and we really needed them to be successful. There was a lot of pressure accompanying the work and it didn't help that I was attending seminary (with my bosses approval) from seven to ten each morning. Furthermore, I had no idea how we were going to reach our sales goal, especially since my marketing budget had shrunk from millions of dollars down to thousands. Trying my best to ignore all the uncertainty, I kept my head down and focused on what I could control and let God worry about the results and my future. Incredibly at the end of that turbulent year, I finished over plan and my revenue had increased while Apple's had continued to dramatically decrease. When people all throughout the company asked how we achieved our results, my answer started with, "By the grace of God." Not everyone said it, but everyone knew it and couldn't deny it; we had all witnessed God do something extraordinary.

Deuteronomy 8:17-18 You may say to yourself, "My power and the strength of my hands have produced this wealth for me." But remember the LORD your God, for it is he who gives you the ability to produce wealth, and so confirms his covenant, which he swore to your forefathers, as it is today.

Ephesians 2:10 For we are God's workmanship, created in Christ Jesus to do good works, which God prepared in advance for us to do.

1 Corinthians 3:7 So neither he who plants nor he who waters is anything, but only God, who makes things grow.

The good works that God has prepared for us to do are meant to bless us and grow His kingdom. Our amazing results help our career and give us opportunities to tell our impressed coworkers about the One who gave us the skills and abilities to achieve. Unfortunately, the success that was intended to catch our coworker's eyes can also capture our adoration. If we don't watch out we can start to worship the blessings of God over Him who blesses and stop giving Him the glory for our success. It can take years of pursuing the next big thing to discover that worldly riches and recognition never provide the satisfaction we long for. Reality hits that our hearts have been kidnapped when our desire for more won't let us enjoy what we have or praise God for what He's given. We can all be tempted to go down this path, which is why Jesus tells us to seek first God's kingdom and righteousness in living out our lives. He promises that if we prioritize God in our work, then He will simply give us the things that everybody else runs after. Experiencing God's faithfulness is how we come to treasure His goodness and begin our journey to love Him with all of our heart. The greater our desire to follow God and His ways, the less interest we'll have in chasing after wealth and what it can buy, and the more we'll praise Him to anyone who will listen.

Luke 12:34 For where your treasure is, there your heart will be also.

Proverbs 21:21 He who pursues righteousness and love finds life, prosperity and honor.

Matthew 6:31-33 So do not worry, saying, 'What shall we eat?' or 'What shall we drink?' or 'What shall we wear?' For the pagans run after all these things, and your heavenly Father knows that you need them. But seek first his kingdom and his righteousness, and all these things will be given to you as well.

Joshua 1:7-8 Be strong and very courageous. Be careful to obey all the law my servant Moses gave you; do not turn from it to the right or to the left, that you may be successful wherever you go. Do not let this Book of the Law depart from your mouth; meditate on it day and night, so that you may be careful to do everything written in it. Then you will be prosperous and successful.

1 Chronicles 29:11-13 Yours, O LORD, is the greatness and the power and the glory and the majesty and the splendor, for everything in heaven and earth is yours. Yours, O LORD, is the kingdom; you are exalted as head over all. Wealth and honor come from you; you are the ruler of all things. In your hands are strength and power to exalt and give strength to all. Now, our God, we give you thanks, and praise your glorious name.

God's knows that most of us will be discouraged from singing His praises in the office, but no one will stop us from worshiping Him by applauding the work of our coworkers. We demonstrate our belief that it's more blessed to give than to receive by honoring the efforts of our coworkers' over our own. Each time we recognize the accomplishments of those God created we bring glory to the Maker of all things. Our encouraging words will get attention in an office used to hearing people put others down to gain recognition for themselves. Subtly, we lead our teammates to the way of salvation by downplaying our role and emphasizing the work of others. By sharing words of affirmation that our ears would love to hear, we soften the hearts of our teammates for the One who wrote the golden rule. It's our genuine excitement for our colleagues' success that sows seeds of God's goodness into our workplace. Everyday, we can touch people for God by simply shaking the hand of a teammate for a job well done.

Acts 20:35b remembering the words the Lord Jesus himself said: 'It is more blessed to give than to receive.'"

Luke 6:31 Do to others as you would have them do to you.

Philippians 2:3-4 Do nothing out of selfish ambition or vain conceit, but in humility consider others better than yourselves. Each of you should look not only to your own interests, but also to the interests of others.

Matthew 5:16 In the same way, let your light shine before men, that they may see your good deeds and praise your Father in heaven.

Questions for Reflection

1. Think of a work success. How did God help you achieve it? Examples:
   - I launched a new program successfully. God gave me a very logical mind.
   - I was way over my sales plan. God blessed me with a fruitful sales territory.
   - I've never had success. I don't really know what I'm great at doing. (We can all feel this way sometimes.)
   - I increased productivity by 20% in operations. God has given me great insight and persistence.

2. Who has God put in your life to help you be successful? Examples:
   - My parents, teachers, and friends.
   - My boss, who is also a great mentor.
   - Nobody. I've done it by myself.
   - My coworkers who help me every day.

3. How can you show your appreciation to the people who've helped you succeed?

Examples:
- I can thank them.
- I can recognize their contribution.
- I don't want to recognize them because they will take all the credit.
- I can recommend them for a promotion.

4. How can you glorify God at work in your achievements?

Examples:
- I can't talk about religion at work.
- I can work in ways that please God so others see that my success is from Him.
- I can tell my coworkers about the God moments in my success.
- I can tell my coworkers that I thank God for getting to work with them.

Made in the USA
Middletown, DE
22 March 2019